T0157390

crash course in *love*

crash course in *love*

STEVE WARD AND JoANN WARD

Pocket Books

New York London

VH1 Books

Toronto Sydney

Pocket Books
A Division of Simon & Schuster, Inc.
1230 Avenue of the Americas
New York, NY 10020

Copyright © 2009 by Steven Ward and JoAnn Ward
VH-1: Music First, *Behind the Music*, and all related titles, logos, and characters are
trademarks of Viacom International Inc.

All rights reserved, including the right to reproduce this book or
portions thereof in any form whatsoever. For information address
Pocket Books Subsidiary Rights Department,
1230 Avenue of the Americas, New York, NY 10020.

First VH-1 Books/Pocket Books trade paperback edition November 2009

POCKET and colophon are registered trademarks of Simon & Schuster, Inc.

For information about special discounts for bulk purchases,
please contact Simon & Schuster Special Sales at 1-866-506-1949
or business@simonandschuster.com.

The Simon & Schuster Speakers Bureau can bring authors to your
live event. For more information or to book an event contact the
Simon & Schuster Speakers Bureau at 1-866-248-3049 or visit our
website at www.simonspeakers.com.

Designed by Ruth Lee Mui

Manufactured in the United States of America

10 9 8 7 6 5 4 3 2 1

Library of Congress Cataloging-in-Publication Data is available.

ISBN 978-1-4767-8798-5
ISBN 978-1-4391-7735-8 (ebook)

contents

introduction

If all the single women out there read this book, we'll be out of business. If you put the principles we share with you here into practice, you will be able to find and attract the right men, develop your connection with them by dating, and form a commitment with one that will last. My mom, JoAnn Ward, and I are Master Matchmakers®. Mom first started matchmaking more than twenty-five years ago by marrying off several family members and friends. It was then that she realized she had a natural instinct for matchmaking and decided to make a living doing it. I grew up watching Mom make one successful match after another and witnessed the passion she has for bringing people together. After graduating college, I spent the summer working at Master Matchmakers to set up a database of our clients and infuse a little more technology into the process. It was 2002 and Mom was still using file folders with Polaroids attached to keep track of everyone! By that point Internet dating had evolved from the obscurity of private chat rooms into the mainstream with commercial international dating websites. People started expecting algorithms and computer science to find them a match from among millions of photos and profiles. But the one thing technology can't replace is personal service, intuition, and attention to detail. Most people flatter themselves online, posting the best possible photos they can find—which are, more often than not, dated. Clients have also complained to us that people they've met online exaggerated their success, lied about their marital status, and misrepresented their height, body type, age, or any number of things. Anyone can throw together an online profile with a flattering photo and have moderate success finding dates, but that's not how they're likely to find the relationship they're looking for. Many singles who use dating sites often just want to date casually and may not necessarily be looking for a relationship, whereas the people we represent make being in a relationship a priority. We provide our clients not only the opportunity to meet hand-selected prospective matches but the ongoing support, direction, and guidance necessary to develop love and a long-lasting relationship.

When I was growing up my mom and dad taught me that with communication, respect, and trust you have the foundation for a great relationship. Over time I've learned how to use these principles to solve the problems that often impede interpersonal relationships. Then, one day in the office that summer after college, I received a phone call from a prospective client. After I explained to her how the service worked and attempted to schedule an interview for her with Mom, she asked if *I* would consider being her matchmaker. She said she wanted a man's perspective and felt I possessed valuable insight that could help her find a man with whom she could build a great relationship. I honestly didn't know if I was ready, willing, or able to take on the challenge and responsibility of being a matchmaker, but I decided to give it a shot. She really appreciated my opinion and insight about her choices in men and, to my surprise, within an hour of meeting her I thought of someone who would be perfect for her. She sensed my confidence and enthusiasm and felt comfortable enough to trust me with her love life and hire me as her matchmaker. I successfully signed her as my first client. The person I had in mind for her didn't want to meet her at first, but I was relentless, and after I talked to him man-to-man and assured him he would not be disappointed, he decided to give it a shot and meet her. The last I heard from him they were engaged to be married—and she's been referring people to our service ever since.

Thus our reputation grew, and our client base grew with it. Thanks to wireless information technology we perfected our personal approach to matchmaking and the Master Matchmakers method. Suddenly Mom and I were meeting three to four dozen singles a month, face-to-face, across seven states and the District of Columbia. We'd meet our would-be clients over a cup of coffee, a cocktail, or a bite to eat and conduct fun yet intense interviews to get to know them as much as possible. We'd come up with potential matches for the people we wanted to work with, taking careful note of everything we discussed. We'd repeat this same interview process and matchmaking cycle with all different sorts of people, from all walks of life, day in and day out. Over time we started noticing more and more correlations. Clients who expressed similar wants, needs, and patterns of behavior also had similar relationship experiences, upbringings, lifestyles, etc. With twenty-five-plus years of combined experience, Mom and I have conducted more than five thousand interviews and arranged more than twenty-five thousand matches. We've sharpened our perception and polished our prowess and evolved from ordinary matchmakers into dating pathologists. We started appearing on TV more and more often as "relationship experts," and finally, in 2007, we caught the attention of some reality-show producers in L.A., who approached us to do our own show.

There are many reality dating shows out there, but none that showcased dating from a male perspective quite like mine. VH1's *Tough Love* changed that. We selected eight women with destructive dating habits to come to L.A. and live in a house together while Mom and I took them through a *Tough Love* boot camp. I was the camp's drill sergeant. We had two months to condition these women and help them through the myriad problems that were plaguing their love lives. From Miss Picky and Miss Bridezilla to Miss Party Girl and Miss Guided, Mom and I had our work cut out for us. None of the women came to the boot camp even close to being ready to have a successful relationship. So we coached them through a series of challenges that taught them to overcome the issues that were causing them one dating disaster and failed relationship after another.

We began season one with an exercise designed to show how visual men are and how much they infer from a first look. (Perceptions and first impressions will either draw men to or prevent them from approaching a woman.) After we gave the women this rude awakening, they faced many other challenges. Each went on to learn important lessons about communication, such as what men would consider to be too much information versus need-to-know information, as well as lessons in sex, like how to be sexy without being slutty, plus many more. Mom and I worked with the women individually and collectively. They were matched up and sent out armed with insight and introspection, equipped to make the most of their opportunities. Some women left boot camp in budding relationships, and some didn't. However, they all learned valuable lessons that should bring them more success in their labors of love. Often throughout the season the women were told things they didn't want to hear, and it got heated from time to time, but that's why it's called tough love. Coming to realizations about yourself and how you live your life isn't very easy and can be very emotional, but it is essential if you want to find the right guy. We tell it like it is, and let our clients know that they may not always like what we're going to say, but it's the truth . . . and sometimes the truth hurts.

Although at times we come off a little harsh, we'd rather seem abrasive than sugarcoat the truth and just tell someone what they want to hear—that's the easy way out. We take a genuine interest in our clients' success. Too many "matchmakers" out there simply run dating factories; they are more interested in just getting people out on dates rather than finding them a good match. We pride ourselves on our screening process and the in-depth consultations we provide all our clients. This process allows us to make the best possible matches. We ask difficult questions because anyone can have chemistry, but without putting things into perspective there's no way to see a relationship clearly. Throughout our many years of making matches and guiding couples from first dates into lasting relationships, we've learned a thing or two. You see many of these lessons and our advice presented on the show, but we wanted to put it all down in one place for you to use as a reference guide. Whether you are single and looking for a man, dating, or already in a relationship, these are important principles that should resonate throughout your life.

There are various stages in a relationship's life cycle, ranging from first identifying a potential connection to moving on from one. Sometimes the whole cycle occurs in an instant; sometimes it occurs over a lifetime. No matter what stage you're in, it's important to know where you want to go so you can figure out a way to get there.

The first stage begins with finding someone. This is pretty simple. You come across a man, have a conversation with him, and allow things to progress to the point where you plan to talk again or, better yet, to see each other again. Most people consider finding the right guy to be the hardest part of forming a great relationship. It *can* be intimidating; looks are often deceiving, and there's always the potential for rejection. But with a positive outlook and a lighthearted attitude, this can actually be the most fun part of forming a great relationship. Next, you start dating. Once you've found a guy you think you could actually have a *real* relationship with, you start dating him. This means going on actual dates and getting to know each other better. Dating is not "hanging out." It's the discovery stage of relationship-building, when you've learned enough about him to start telling your friends and family about him and to become exclusive. Then you begin the developing stage. You introduce each other to family and friends and make accommodations in your lives for each other. After you've settled into exclusivity, you begin strengthening your commitment. You welcome the responsibility of managing each other's expectations and growing together, both as a couple and as individuals, and within the framework of your commitment. The final stage in the life cycle of your relationship is keeping and maintaining the relationship. You mature your connection and focus on making the relationship exciting, enjoying life together, and consciously *not* growing apart. The end game for us as Master Matchmakers is not necessarily marriage, but a healthy, happy, monogamous relationship in which both people are determined to remain committed to each other. We believe in marriage as an institution, no different than religion. It helps to reinforce commitment, bridge families, create traditions, and strengthen a community. But marriage is not for everyone. As long as you are in a committed relationship based on communication, respect, and trust, we consider you a success. To help you along your path to love, we've come up with the following principles and advice to guide you through the most important aspects of finding and creating your own healthy, happy relationship.

dating

Women often say, "I can't find a good man," or "There are no good guys out there." Well, I beg to differ. There are "good" single guys everywhere, and like you, they're looking for someone. Many of them are in situations or stages of their own lives that are preventing them from realizing their full potential, and they just haven't met the right woman, the one who will inspire them to be all they can be. The key is changing how you look at life and opening your mind to the possibility of meeting someone you would least expect, in a place where you would least expect it. Once you connect with a man who interests you, the goal is to make plans to see him again with the intention of dating—or, at the very least, to speak again soon. This requires exchanging contact information and being proactive. In this day and age, women, like men, must seize the moment and make their desires known. Dating is the discovery stage of relationship-building. It's the time when you are supposed to learn more about him, but also—and equally important—it's when he can learn about you so you can both determine if there is a connection. Love requires an alternating current. To harness and generate love, the connection must flow both ways. A direct current or a one-way connection is considered lust, not love.

finding and communicating

don't be weird. Remember, what we consider "weird" is a matter of perception, but there are things that most people would generally agree are weird, things that would be a turnoff for someone you are on a date with or meeting for the first time in a social situation. Being weird also depends on context. For example, if you meet someone at a Halloween party and say, "I'm a vampire," that's not weird. However, if you meet someone at a speed-dating event and tell him you are a vampire, that's just weird. Keep in mind that what is "normal" for you may not be normal for someone else. So keep the questionable comments to yourself for now. There is nothing to be gained by saying something that might seem bizarre to a guy you are dating. A strange comment that might amuse you will probably annoy him. You should not look to get a reaction or instigate an argument.

the first step to getting what you want is knowing what you want. You shouldn't be picky; you should just know exactly what you're looking for *subjectively*, and it will be much easier to find. Imagine yourself looking into a crystal ball and seeing your love life two years from now. In order to get what you want, you must first visualize it. You are the only one who can make it happen, but you have to know what you want before you can go out and try to get it. Any pursuit without a goal is an endless pursuit. First, set your sights on immediate, attainable goals. Then establish longer-term goals and create a road map in your mind to guide you in achieving the life and relationship you've always desired. There are many ways to get where you want to go, but you have to know where you're going before you take off.

if you are looking to meet the right guy, you must keep in mind that eligible single people are everywhere, and often in places that you never think to look! If you spot someone you're attracted to and think that he's either acknowledged you or signaled an interest of his own, you have to be confident enough to close the physical gap between you and casually ask an innocent question. Personally, my favorite question is, "Are you single?" No matter what the response is, you should always say politely and cutely, "Well you shouldn't be." And smile. Try it. It works.

this is what I call the Michael Jordan rule: You will miss one hundred percent of the shots you don't take. If you take a shot with a guy, at least you stand a chance of making it, but if you don't even bother, you are guaranteed not to find love. You have to take a chance if there is to be any possibility of success. If you see a guy at a bar, a coffee shop, the cafeteria at work, online, in line, or on the street and you think he's cute, go and talk to him, ask him a question. What do you have to lose? He may be a great guy or he may not, but if you don't give it a shot you'll never find out. If you approach a guy in public, it's not likely he's going to accost you for saying hello. The worst that could happen is he'll say he's not interested. Consider it his loss.

being single and seeking a relationship is like warfare, and every date is another battle. Treat dating like it's a mission you must accomplish or a fight you have to win. It is essential to have some kind of strategy with a reasonable goal, and some idea of how you intend to execute your game plan. If you are in a rut—you've asked all your friends to set you up; you've reached out to everyone you know who has a single friend—and you really need to branch out, come up with a plan. Join an intramural team, a club, or an office sports team. Try taking a class at a local university, change gyms, volunteer, shop at a different grocery store or mall, find a hobby that can be done in a group. Figure out a strategy for overcoming your challenge, and then go do it!

always try to be calm, cool, and collected when you are with a guy. You don't want to seem awkward, anxious, or nervous, even if you are. Treat being on a date like walking into a bank or through airport security: If you start acting nervous, the people around you might get nervous themselves. If you seem at ease and relaxed, he will feel the same way. Always give off good energy.

know your audience. Be careful of what you say and when you say it. It is best not to bring up potentially controversial or sensitive subjects with someone you've just met. You don't want to talk about religion, politics, past relationships, personal finance, or anything negative whatsoever. You can't possibly know how he feels about these sensitive subjects, so at this point you should try to steer clear of them. He could have a brother serving in the Middle East or a close friend who had an abortion—you just don't know yet. Even if you accidentally trigger a reaction by touching on something sensitive, do an evasive maneuver and change the subject quickly. At this early stage you should be trying to feel out your audience and getting to know him. As things progress, you can show him that you have been paying attention when something comes up that is related to a topic you've already discussed by making a reference to something he told you earlier. He'll see and appreciate the fact that you've been listening. If you demonstrate to him that you are aware and present, it will have a profound effect.

men like a good challenge; it's in their nature. They love the thrill of the hunt. It's okay to make him earn a relationship with you, but don't let him know you're making him work for it. If he is really interested he'll do what it takes to see you. However, you must manage his expectations and realize that the harder you make him work in order to be with you, the more he is going to expect from you. This technique is a double-edged sword: To the victor go the spoils, and the harder he fights, the more of a prize he is going to expect. Make sure that you will live up to the expectations you create, if he lives up to yours.

less is more. This is a practical tip that applies to many things in the dating world, but it especially applies to makeup and perfume (though not, it should be noted, to clothes). No guy I know wants to date a member of KISS, or someone who looks completely different when they wake up in the morning or step out of the shower than they did the night before. So keep the makeup toned down. The same applies to perfume—don't give your date a headache with an assault on his sinuses. A little fragrance and makeup go a long way. Mom's advice to women who are preparing to go out with a man for the first time—or for the fiftieth time—is to moisturize your legs after you shave, do not tattoo on your eyebrows, do not use lip pencil (no matter what the girl at the makeup counter tells you), and no body glitter!

wear something that is appropriate for the date, and if you're not sure what you're doing or where you're going, just ask him. You don't want to dress for a fancy dinner when you're really getting burgers and taking a walk through the park, which could end up being a blistering hike in high heels that you definitely won't enjoy. Most men couldn't tell you what couture clothing is, and most don't appreciate designer shoes, either. If wearing those things makes you feel good about yourself, then you should wear them around family, friends, and colleagues, or when you are sure that it is appropriate attire for a date. Generally speaking, men want to see a woman wear something that simply flatters her figure, is coordinated well, and isn't too loud or cumbersome.

learn to laugh at yourself. No one wants to date a woman who takes herself too seriously. The purpose of entering into a relationship is to enhance your life and your partner's life. A relationship should make your life better. It should bring more happiness and fun into your life. A guy who is dating you is not going to be dating you for long if you are consistently negative or giving off bad vibes. Don't focus on how bad your day was at work and what a jerk your boss is, or how much money you've lost in the stock market. No one wants to date Negative Nancy. The best way to diffuse a negative situation is to make light of it. Be positive, be happy, and don't be afraid to laugh!

never be neutral. You should have opinions. You don't have to be argumentative, but always agreeing with a man is not going to make him more attracted to you. Dating a woman who always agrees with you is boring. Be an individual. Make sure he knows that you are open-minded and receptive to other points of view, but you are not afraid of expressing your own opinion. You could easily end up in a debate if you disagree with your guy, but don't let it get that far or that serious. Joke with him about your difference of opinion. Banter with him, and keep it witty and light. Words can easily become twisted, especially in a conversation between a man and a woman who are just starting to date and getting to know each other. Both people will be inclined to want to demonstrate their intelligence or knowledge of a particular subject to impress each other—you can do this without picking a fight. Remember: Banter is good, arguments are bad.

don't hate the player, hate the game.

I'm referring to the 7, 8, 9 Rule. Most guys use a scale of 1 to 10 to "rate" a girl or to describe her to someone else. It's shallow and superficial, of course, but try looking at it in a different way. It's a sliding scale that differs for each guy. Guys see it like this: A 7 is a girl who they would take home for a night; an 8 is a girl who they would date and introduce to friends; and a 9 is a girl they would take home to meet the family. And let's face it—no one is a 10. A 10 might be someone a guy feels lucky just to be around. One man's 10 is someone else's 9; the scale is subjective. Have you ever said to a friend, "What does he see in her?" Well, your 6 may be his 8. Everyone has a different perspective. These numbers aren't based on your looks alone (unless he hasn't had a chance to talk to you). Your personality and how you are perceived are important factors as well. By changing a man's impression, you can change where he places you on his scale. This is why it's important to always be the best you can be. You always want to be your man's 9. Your stock can rise in a man's eyes if you take this advice to heart and follow these principles. The elasticity of this scale is what makes the *Tough Love* boot camp work; the women on the show came into our boot camp in no shape to be in a relationship, but after working with me and my mom they were ready to find love. They rose up the scale.

have a sip instead of a shot. When a guy sees a girl tear through a bar like a tornado in Texas, slammin' shots like she hasn't had a drink in five years, the only thing he's thinking is that she's going to be a sloppy mess who will probably need a ride home at the end of the night. Be aware that the more you drink, the less respect he'll have for you. You will also be a lot more likely after several drinks to start divulging too much information. Stay in control. Even if you're not taking shots, exercise caution—you don't want to go overboard with wine, beer, or cocktails, either. Dating is supposed to be fun, but you have to drink responsibly or you could end up going further than you intend and generally making decisions that you'll regret later.

try to stand out. Don't be a wallflower. Come out of the woodwork. Find a happy medium between crazy-loud and shy-boring. Guys need to know you are there if they are going to ask you out or talk to you. Women's roles have changed, and these days if you want to meet a great man, you must stand out and be recognized. This is related to the law of natural selection—the process by which species with traits that enable them to successfully compete for mates will survive and reproduce in greater numbers, ensuring the perpetuation of those favorable traits in succeeding generations. This might explain why women have become so prominent in the worlds of business, politics, sports, and entertainment in recent years. When it comes to dating, especially in densely populated cities like New York, L.A., and Chicago, it is all about survival of the fittest. Only those who are best adapted to the conditions will be able to survive, reproduce, and thrive. So make sure you stand out. That doesn't mean you have to be loud and obnoxious, or obvious about drawing attention to yourself. You can be seen and not heard, and still attract a man's attention.

This is a perfect example of when body language is just as important as personal style and verbal communication: If you want to attract the attention of a man, you must be able to make eye contact. You don't want to stare or make the guy feel like you're goofing on him, but it's essential to make eye contact to initiate a connection. You also want to smile as much as possible, and be conscious of it. If you are in a room with a man you are interested in, or walking into a room where you know he is standing, make sure you have a smile on your face. Also, walk with good posture—keep your head up, shoulders back, and chest out, and walk confidently. If you slouch or slump you are going to project a sense of tiredness or unhappiness. You must project positive energy to attract a man.

don't judge a book by its cover. This may seem hypocritical, because men do this all the time, but men are much more visual than women. It's always been this way, and it's meant to be this way. Men have always been expected to be the ones to make the approach, and the only thing they have to go on when approaching a woman they've never met is looks. Even though society has come a long way in terms of gender roles, we have to recognize that some of the more traditional expectations still exist. So when it comes to first impressions, try not to make snap judgments, like many men do. Whether you are looking for a guy or on a date, remember that you're only scratching the surface when you first meet a man. Give him a chance to reveal himself instead of sizing him up and shutting him down in the first two minutes. First impressions are critical, but don't jump to conclusions.

Stay open, receptive, and interested. The minute you shut down, put up your guard, and disconnect, he will, too. For example, you may meet a guy who has two strikes against him in the first five minutes of conversation. For instance, maybe he's shorter than your usual type, and you *think* that he makes less money than you. Don't dismiss him. He may be a great person, and may even appreciate you more and treat you better than a taller, wealthier man would. He may be more successful than he leads you to believe, or have the passion and drive to be very successful in the future. The point is, you don't know, so don't make assumptions just yet. This is especially important for women who have a certain "type." If you are still single and looking for that type hasn't been working, it may be time to change the kind of man you're looking for or dating. Your true love could come in an unfamiliar package that you never expected to receive, so keep an open mind!

women may not want to hear this, but it's the truth, so I'm going to lay it out there: Most men we've come across in our years of matchmaking tell us that they would rather date a fit girl who they consider less pretty than an overweight girl who may have prettier features. This tendency relates to the law of natural selection that I mentioned earlier. Men will subconsciously select a healthier woman. The principle works both ways, of course—most women aren't seeking a man with a beer gut, just as men tend not to choose heavier women. There's nothing wrong with curves in the right places, or a little junk in the trunk, as long as you are eating right, staying healthy, and getting some exercise. So if you appear unhealthy, maybe this fact will motivate you to do something about it. Being more attracted to a healthier person is just human nature and something to be aware of when you're trying to meet your match.

never fish for compliments. If a guy thinks you look good, he will tell you. Always put your best foot forward, and be confident. If you feel good about yourself, you won't need someone to reassure you. You will already know that you look good and will probably get validation in the form of positive body language from others in the room. Show off your best assets, especially your intellect. Promote your physical features as well as your brains, show him everything you have to offer, but don't fish for compliments. If you do he'll think you're insecure, self-centered, and needy.

don't devalue or degrade yourself. Don't be self-deprecating. If a guy compliments you, accept the compliment graciously by simply thanking him, and offer one back in return if it's appropriate. Project a sense of confidence and self-esteem. Insecurity is a big turnoff; he'll wonder what made you insecure and if you're carrying around a lot of baggage. Remember, if he says something nice it's because he means it. Guys are pretty simple; they usually just say what they mean.

A tip from JoAnn: A plain old "thank you" is the best way to accept a compliment. That's all you need to say. If someone compliments your hair, don't say, "Oh, no. It doesn't look good today. It's so frizzy in this humidity." Or if you get a compliment on a dress you are wearing, don't say, "I always feel fat in this dress." Don't expose your insecurities. If he thinks you look good, thank him for telling you! If you tell him he's wrong, he won't bother complimenting you again. And if it's appropriate, say something nice in return, like, "Thank you! And I love your tie; that's a great color on you."

don't sell yourself short. If a guy appears to be into you, don't give him reasons why he shouldn't be. Check your baggage at the door, or at least stow it in an overhead compartment or under the seat in front of you. When you are first dating a guy it's not a good idea to unload all your problems, demons, and struggles on him all at once. If something negative *does* come up in conversation, keep the discussion light, and focus on how it impacted you in a positive way. This advice is important, so please don't take it for granted. I'm sure you'll agree the door swings both ways here. We live in a world where everyone expects instant gratification. We obsess if people don't respond to our texts right away, or if our schedules prevent us from seeing each other when we want. When you're starting to date a guy it's critical to focus on how it will work, instead of why it won't. Whether you live on opposite sides of the city or in different cities altogether, or you have pets or children who need to be considered, or you're saddled with allergies, phobias, or meddlesome exes or family members, you must spin the situation in such a way that he thinks, *This is how it could work*, rather than *This is why it won't*.

close the gap. Flirting is all about closing the physical gap between you and another person, indicating that you want to approach him or inviting him to approach you. Moving closer is the key factor in showing someone you are interested. If you lean in while he's talking to you it shows that you are listening and interested in what he's saying, and that you are comfortable being physically close to him. If you are sitting back with your arms crossed, looking over his shoulder while he's speaking to you, he'll think you don't care. So be a flirt, because flirting, when done correctly, is incredibly sexy. Tease your man, let him know that you are interested in him sexually, and when the time is right, it will happen. Enticing him and building that anticipation will just make it better in the end. Focus on flirting first, and when you are both comfortable and ready, intimacy will come naturally and be more enjoyable for both of you. When you're flirting with a guy, whether it is on a date or just in a bar or at a party, here are some important tips to remember:

5 Do's in Flirting

1. **Smile.** Nothing lets a person know you're picking up what they're putting down better than a smile. If you're happy, he's happy!

2. **Make eye contact.** Making and maintaining eye contact shows a guy you're focused, confident, and interested in what he is saying and doing. The eyes tell all.

3. **Flatter.** There's no clearer indication that you have a romantic interest in someone than a compliment.

4. **Take charge.** Take the conversation where you want it to go. If you expect him to call, give him your number. If you want to call him, ask for his.

5. **Act gracefully.** If he's unavailable or uninterested, maintain your poise and just pretend you never started flirting in the first place.

5 Don'ts in Flirting:

1. **Don't make it too obvious.** Be subtle, but get your point across. You don't have to be over-the-top; subtle indications are the most effective way to let him know that you're attracted and interested.

2. **Don't stare.** It's important to let the person know you're interested, but it's equally important not to make him uncomfortable.

3. **Don't overdo it.** A simple compliment will advance your efforts much further than a fabricated pickup line.

4. **Don't flirt with others simultaneously.** It will confuse a man and bewilder him if you're flirting with him and others at the same time. Keep your eyes on the prize.

5. **Don't feign interest.** For men, flirting is often realized in hindsight. If you flirt and then act uninterested, he won't pursue you. Keep your signals consistent.

if you want him to kiss you, get closer. You don't have to throw yourself at him, but send him some signals. Square your shoulders to him, make eye contact, maybe even gaze at his lips. Don't just play with your hair and let your eyes wander. Guys get nervous, too, and often will show it by being timid—or the opposite, by being overzealous. Some guys may make a move too quickly, or not quickly enough, when they're nervous. It's your job to guide him in making the connection, and to manage his expectations. If a guy is a little too pushy for your taste, don't hold it against him; just politely tell him the time isn't right, or that you're not interested at all. My mom always told me, "You can't blame a guy for trying, but when a girl says no, it means no." If you want him to make a move, try to draw him out of his shell. However, if a guy is just too shy to kiss you, sometimes you have to take the bull by the horns and kiss him yourself. If you are going to initiate the kiss, make sure you are positive that he wants it; don't set yourself up for rejection. You should be able to read his body language and know if he will be receptive, but be aware that if he hasn't made a move and doesn't seem like he is going to, he may just not be into you. Keep in mind that it is possible a guy won't try to sleep with you in the first week or even month that you are dating. He may be taking the relationship seriously and getting to know you before becoming intimate. Don't make it awkward by being too aggressive; just be aware and trust your instincts. Mom says, "P.S.: Always have a mint available."

keep the past in the past. You want a man to embrace who you are today, not who you were in the past. In other words, keep your skeletons (along with your exes) in the closet. For example, in season one of *Tough Love* Arian revealed in a two-minute speed-dating session that she used to be an exotic dancer. That was not the time or the place to reveal a detail like that about her past. It's okay to embrace the things you've done, but think about how a guy might react before you reveal too much and scare him off. On the first date, does he really need to know that you've been arrested for public urination? Probably not.

there is no room for double standards in dating. You know the expression—do unto others as you would have them do unto you. This especially applies to dating. If you won't consider a relationship with an older man, don't expect a younger man to consider a relationship with you. You are not the exception to the rule, so don't hold others to a standard you can't maintain yourself. If we were paid ten dollars for every time a woman told us she looks younger than her age, we would be living the sweet life on the beach in Southern California right now. We take issue with cougar relationships because those May-December situations usually never last. Younger men date older women for several reasons: 1) Older women are perceived as being more mature, experienced, and comfortable with their sexuality than younger women; 2) Older women are more secure emotionally and financially, and are generally more independent than younger women; and 3) Older women don't normally expect a relationship with a younger man to last, thus relieving a lot of the pressure men normally face.

be positive and look your best. Most singles claim to know in the blink of an eye whether or not there is "chemistry." Others may allow it to develop over time, but people invariably judge each other based on appearances, so it's critical to consider how others see you and to put some thought into your style and the signals it sends. Make sure the image you project reflects how you want to be perceived. Don't expect him to think you are cerebral and serious if you are wearing a tube top, a short skirt, and five-inch translucent heals. The classier and sexier you look in your own eyes, the better the perception he'll have of you.

first impressions matter most, so don't waste your first impression. It's nearly impossible to change someone's perception if you make a bad first impression. Not only should you be aware of what you are wearing, you have to be aware of the signals that you send by how you carry yourself. Here are five tips you should always remember when meeting a guy for the first time:

1. **Smile:** Be happy! If you are smiling, he'll probably smile right back.
2. **Listen:** Guys notice if you remember something they said earlier. No man wants to feel like his date isn't paying attention.
3. **Focus:** Be present. Don't play with your phone or have your hands in your pockets. The only time you should mind your phone is if your kids are

with a new babysitter or you are an on-call medical professional. Using your phone on a date or when someone has just approached you is a turn-off for anyone. It will make a man feel uneasy and unimportant. If he senses that you are preoccupied, he'll assume you're uninterested and will move on.

4. **Be positive:** Be open. Be agreeable. If he suggests a restaurant that you haven't been to, don't protest. Go, and be excited about trying something new. Dating is a great opportunity to broaden your horizons and experience things that you haven't had the opportunity to experience before.

5. **Be sexy:** Sexy to a man means confident, fun, and approachable. If you feel sexy, he'll sense it and will respond. Let him give it his best shot, and then decide if you're interested.

wear your underwear under what you wear. All too often women let their bra and underwear creep out from under their clothes. Most of the time you don't even realize it. You have to be conscious of this whether it is your bra or panties or both. When men see underwear a red alert goes off in their minds. Most men think about sex often, and this will make your date's mind wander in that direction for sure. Even the hint of your underwear beneath your clothes, that little line, will make a man's mind wander. If you're not sure where you want the relationship to go, be mindful of this distraction.

never underestimate the power of the "wow" factor. If you took guitar lessons as a kid and you're great at *Rock Band*, show him your talent. If your dad is a cop and taught you how to fire a gun, let him know. Maybe you grew up with brothers who are die-hard football fans and you know everything there is to know about the game. This sort of thing will impress a man. You don't want to brag; just show him the unique qualities that make you different from other women. Remember the law of natural selection. If he thinks you are special and different from the women he usually meets, he will be more interested in making the most out of your connection.

if you have a thing for bad boys, try to look for the ones who were released for good behavior. It is always better to date a bad boy who has been reformed than to have to try to reform one yourself. The way a bad boy usually learns his lesson is by taking for granted and losing someone who loved him very much. Don't be fooled by the bad boy who is only pretending to be reformed. Get to know him before you jump in. Make him realize that you are worth settling down for, and make an honest man out of him.

always maintain your dignity. If you feel threatened by another woman, the last thing you want to do is show it in front of the man you are with. It indicates a lack of confidence, which is a critical ingredient when you are trying to get a man to perceive you as sexy and desirable. Be classy, and take the high road. Here's a suggestion: The first time you see his eyes wander or notice his attention drawn to another woman, make it clear that you see him noticing another woman and that you like people-watching, too. Tell him you find it amusing and wonder what that other person's story is. If you catch him doing it a second time, whether on the same date or on a different night, call him out on it. If it happens a third time, tell him, "I don't think you've caught me looking at any one of the number of men who have checked me out during our dates, so do me a favor and don't let me

catch you checking out other women again. Thanks."
You've either turned him off or are not able to keep his
attention. If he continues to let his eyes wander, cut
your losses and move on.

communication

Communication is fundamental to finding, developing, and keeping a relationship strong. Without communication, there could be no relationship. There are many different levels and forms of communication, from electronic to verbal to body language. A simple miscommunication can be disastrous for a new relationship. In the very beginning stages of forming and developing a connection, clear, concise, and direct communication is critical. It's just as easy to raise flags when you say too much too soon as it is when you don't say enough. Communication is a slippery slope, and people have very different styles of communication. Some people can express themselves easily, but others prefer to imply what they mean instead. Some people just don't communicate at all, which is the death of any relationship. Don't bother interpreting what someone else is trying to say. It's much better to just ask them to explain what they mean more clearly. As a woman, you should follow his lead in communicating, just as you would when dancing. If he is a little shy and reserved at first, don't feel like you have to fill the lulls in the conversation by going on about yourself. It's better to try to spark an interesting conversation on a compelling topic than to just start talking about whatever's on your mind. If you're having trouble getting a man to talk it's usually easiest to get him talking about what he does for a living and why he went into that field. A man will usually have no problem talking about hobbies, sports, or interests he is passionate about outside of work. Family is also relatively easy to talk about, but when you start getting into religion, politics, past relationships, or subjects of that nature you are drifting into dangerous territory. In dating, no matter what communication style the other person demonstrates, as the comfort level rises between you the communication will become easier and less inhibited. Communication will broaden and deepen as the connection develops. Even in a long-term committed relationship, communication is the most important tool you can use to reinforce the connection.

never underestimate the power of a woman's intuition, and never overestimate the power of a man's. Don't expect him to be as intuitive as you are. In fact, don't expect him to be intuitive at all. If you want to know something about him, ask. There are clever ways to find out what you want to know without prying: You can ask someone who might know him; you can try flanking the subject you are interested in and leading the conversation in a gentle and nonaggressive way. This is important because if he feels like he's getting the third degree, being put on the spot, or cornered in any way, he'll shut down immediately and his ego will take over. If you want to find out how a guy feels about a sensitive subject, try to feel him out first. For example, say you're more spiritual and sense that he may be more religious. This could become a problem in the future, so you want to make sure you don't waste each other's time, but you don't want to get too deep too soon, either. So, start talking about things you like to do; mention reading or watching movies. Tell him about books you've read recently, or movies you've seen. Ask him whether he ever read or saw *The Da Vinci Code*. Then you can say, casually, "I didn't understand all the dogma 'cause I'm not that religious. What did you think of it?" If you find yourself grappling with any uncertainty that really bothers you and he's not taking your bait, you may just have to ask him what it is you want to know. Make sure when asking something directly about a sensitive subject to do it in a way that doesn't alienate him, and don't be afraid of his response or read too much into it. Remember, forcing out information that might be too much too soon may impact your perception of him and your opinion of the relationship. You must condition yourself not to draw premature conclusions.

actions speak louder than words. Insinuation is just as much a form of art as dance is. Learn to read a person like a book. Body language is as fundamental to the dating world as Latin is to the romance languages, and figuring out how to read the body language of the man you are with is essential to building the relationship. If his eyes are wandering, or if he's checking his watch or fiddling with his phone or can't sit still, you're losing his attention, and you're losing it fast. To capture his attention again, you have to do or say something bold. Shift the focus of conversation suddenly to something that you know will engage him, like his favorite baseball team or a mutual friend.

at the end of a date, most men, if they at least find the woman physically attractive, will try to make some physical contact—even if they don't have an interest in seeing the woman again. Beware the ass-out hug with a pat on the back, or the cheek-bump kiss-on-the-cheek fake-out, or the handshake. These are sure signs of disinterest. A real hug with a rub on the back is a good thing. Here are five actions to watch for that will help you determine if a man is physically attracted to you:

1. He makes physical contact with you on more than one instance during the date, like putting his hand on your back when he lets you go through a door first.

2. He maintains eye contact throughout the entire date and is not easily distracted.

3. You notice him observing you when you are not engaged in conversation.

4. He sits up straight, leans in toward you, and has his arms uncrossed.

5. He laughs and smiles, and he notices when other men look at you. And Mom always says if he hugs you tight and holds on it's because he doesn't want to let you go, and he's definitely interested. I couldn't agree more.

be honest about your job. It's okay to talk up what you do if it's not all that fascinating, but there's a fine line between right and wrong. The janitor who says he's a "master of custodial art" is not quite as dishonest as the life-insurance salesman who says he's an investment banker. Don't be ashamed of your job. No matter what you do, whether you love it or hate it, find a way to make it seem interesting, and speak about it positively and with enthusiasm. If the person asks you more than three questions about what you do, consider this mission accomplished and move on to other subjects like personal interests, family, etc. Discussing your careers is the easiest way to start a conversation, but if the whole night becomes just about your job, then it has turned into a networking event instead of a date.

everyone has a different relationship with money. Don't assume that the guy you're dating looks at a dollar bill the same way you do. The topic of finances is not something you should discuss too early in the relationship, and don't judge a guy by whether or not you think he has money. Don't be a gold digger! It's shallow, and guys don't want to feel used. When you bring up money on a date you will either sound like you're bragging or like you're broke. It's a double-edged sword. There are ways to let the other person know you're financially secure without saying a word or showing off. Never discuss money or the cost of anything in dollars and cents during the initial stage of connecting with someone. Consciously avoid talking about it. Whenever the question of the bill arises—the amount of a charge, the cost of the tickets, the price of gas, etc.—just be generous and gracious.

Whether he picks up the tab for a two-hundred-dollar dinner or a two-dollar ice-cream cone, thank him very sincerely. Offering to pick up the tab, split the bill, or leave the tip will go a long way with a man. If you offer to chip in and he doesn't let you, just thank him. But if he lets you pick up the tab or splits it with you and you just started dating, it's not a good sign. It could mean he's cheap, strapped, or just not interested—none of which bodes well for you. If he lets you leave the tip he might just be testing you to see if you would put any skin in the game. Men want to be generous because they decide to be, not because it is expected. Guys can easily be rubbed the wrong way by women who expect generosity. It immediately sends red flags and raises the gold-digger alert. This is why showing appreciation and making the offer to contribute go a long way. Often women find themselves in a position where they make more money than the guy they are dating. If you want to do something nice for him and treat him to a date, do it nonchalantly and discreetly. Men have to feel like they can provide, and for some men it can be emasculating if they can't spend money on a woman. You should really appreciate it if a man with limited resources goes out of his way to plan an inexpensive, but thoughtful, date.

you should text only need-to-know information that doesn't require dialogue—things like "I'm running late," "I can't make it," or "I'm married." Text messaging is not intended for conversation. People forget that's what the phone was created for in the first place. You should text only to convey an important piece of information or to make a specific request that can be answered with one sentence. When it comes to dating, it's hard enough to write something creative and witty on a greeting card when you have a limited amount of blank space. It's even harder to convey tone, demeanor, and inflection in 160 characters or less. On top of all that, most men are not as eloquent as John Adams or Cyrano de Bergerac. When first getting to know someone, text as little as possible. It is too easy for a text message to be misinterpreted or misunderstood. Even simply not responding quickly enough can send the wrong signals. A good general rule is don't text 'til there's sex. At least that way there's some intimacy established, and both people should feel less insecure if the other isn't as responsive or expressive as they would like. This rule also applies to Facebook, Twitter, MySpace, Match.com, or any other form of social networking. I can't tell you how many times we've counseled men and women who have come to conclusions about people they are seeing based on who their Facebook friends are, the pictures on their MySpace page, or the mere fact that their last login on Match.com was after their last date. We suggest that you ignore someone else's online social-networking behavior under all circumstances. Let me be clear: Ignore it *no matter what*. Imagine if your date dissected every post, picture, or comment on your page. Men don't trust other men, and any interaction they see between you and other men will be threatening on some level. They may not feel that guys you are talking to online are a direct threat to your connection, but they may feel that you are keeping your options open, playing the field, or trying to make them jealous. If you start seeing someone exclusively, you should make it known on your social-networking sites, and deactivate online dating accounts altogether.

if you're addicted to your cell phone and can't help texting your friends with every development throughout the day, you must hold back with the man you are dating and observe the three-text rule. That means if you must text him at all, go ahead and send him one message. If you do not receive a response, wait until you can talk to him and give him a call. When you speak with him, don't mention the unacknowledged text, and get to the point of why you called. If you don't reach him, leave a voice mail with your question and, again, do *not* mention the unacknowledged text. If you are in a situation where you cannot talk on the phone but you must communicate with him, go ahead and send another text—just don't mention the first one. Under no circumstances should you send him a third message if he has not responded to your first two texts. Either call him if it is something urgent or put the phone down and walk away. Don't become a text offender. If he isn't texting you back there is a reason for it, whether you like it or not. The last thing you want is to seem obsessive, impatient, or anxious. He may just be busy, or maybe he was occupied with something when he got the first text and forgot to respond, or he may not be into you. If you've left one or two voice mails and sent one or two texts and he doesn't get back to you in three days, go on with your life as if he never existed. Make your third attempt your final attempt to reach him, and make it clear you're leaving the ball in his court. Don't give ultimatums. Don't make threats. But don't close the door on him reconnecting in your last message because if he is actually interested and there is a legitimate reason he didn't get back to you, you'll never hear it. If he resurfaces and his explanation for being out of touch seems reasonable, give him a reprieve—just this once. If it happens again you've got yourself a guy with communication issues, and we suggest you spare yourself the agony of constantly struggling to reach him.

women tend to give away too much information when they meet a guy they are actually attracted to, usually because they are nervous, they are very interested in the guy, or they don't think he will judge them. But in reality, men are always judging women in the getting-to-know-you stage. TMI is a turnoff. If you tell a guy your entire life story on the first date, he's going to think you are insecure, self-centered, or testing him to see if he can handle the baggage in your life. On the other hand, if a "smooth operator" tells a woman his life story, he is usually setting the stage for a sexual advance. The number one reason women give for not wanting to sleep with a man right away is, "But I don't even know you." If he's already revealed everything to you, his response will be, "What do you mean? You know everything about me." If you're dealing with a smooth operator, head him off at the pass.

Drop hints that you won't be sleeping with him that night, but don't be too obvious about it. You can say things like, "I'm having so much fun getting to know you. I'd stay out later if I didn't have to get up so early for work tomorrow." Don't make it seem like you're following a rule and he's no exception; men need to feel special. If you're not interested in sleeping with him that night, but you might consider it in the future, you have to be sure not to make him feel rejected—especially after he has clearly expressed that he wants you. Make him feel exceptional . . . but don't make an exception. If you're dealing with a guy who seems very innocent—maybe he's a bit shy or reserved and he's giving you TMI—he's probably just nervous. Not all guys are trying to get you into bed with this strategy; just be wary of the ones who are. Try to relate and share experiences if your guy is just nervous, but make sure you're not divulging too much yourself. If there is instant chemistry, a strong connection, and a sense of mutual respect and trust, the gloves can come off. Do whatever you like. Be mindful of rushing a connection with someone, though. Make sure you have the same goals. You may want a relationship when all he wants is to get into your pants. Before you're intimate with him, be clear about what you expect going forward.

the tmi rule also applies to your profile on an online dating site. If you fill out every detail about yourself on that profile, he has nothing to look forward to discovering about you! Some women may think, *If I put everything on there and he still messages me, he must really like me.* Wrong! Guys are visual creatures. Most men are only looking at your pictures, and if one likes what he sees he'll instantly skim your profile for sensational buzzwords like *sexy, fun, passionate*, etc., before choosing to read it. Other than how turned on he was by the photos and whether or not he noticed any buzzwords, he will consider exactly how much you write. When a man logs in, he typically looks at dozens of profiles at a time, and he'll usually spend no more than just a few seconds per profile on average. If he has to read more information on your profile than he does with the others, he will lose interest and move on. Subconsciously, he is realizing that looking at your profile requires more work, and to him that means that being with you would require more work than it would with other women. Keep the profile brief: two or three sentences, tops, and light on the really personal details. Let a man get to know about you the old-fashioned way—in person. Tell him about your career, your family, and your life after you've met face-to-face.

conversation is a dialogue, not a monologue. It's meant to be a two-way street. You can't get to know a guy without letting him talk. So try not to dominate the conversation by talking about yourself the whole time when you first meet a guy. You may notice that he's losing interest by observing his body language. If you see this happening, switch gears and slip into interviewer mode. But be careful not to polarize the situation by interrogating him. When first establishing a connection and getting to know a guy, use the approach commonly known as the KISS method: Keep It Simple, Stupid. Throw out softball questions that you know he can hit. Men don't want to answer or discuss challenging or complex questions with a woman they don't know very well. Things can easily escalate into an argument, and then you'll both be defensive and standoffish for the rest of the date. The ego will take over, and it's downhill from there. Once a strong connection has been established, though, it's okay to discuss more thought-provoking issues. Or you can ask something like, "Now that Michael Vick is reinstated in the NFL, do you think that leaves the door open for any hardened criminal to make millions of dollars a year in salary and endorsements?" That is the kind of question that would impress a guy. The more thought-provoking questions are not likely to put a man on the defensive once you've already clicked.

approach everything with an open mind, especially if you are faced with doing something that you've never tried before or are unaccustomed to. There are few turnoffs greater than a bad attitude. If you are doing something outside of your comfort zone, try to at least be positive about it. Men don't expect you to compete with them; they just want you to try. When a man asks a woman to try something out of the ordinary it's usually because he thinks she is exceptionally educated, informed, or experienced, and he wants to impress her. Let him strut like a peacock and show off a little. If you're not impressed you should realize this might be the best he can do. At the very least, look at it as a learning experience and try to have some fun; otherwise, the guy is going to think you're rigid, high-maintenance, and uncompromising. You should be flexible and accommodating, not negative and stuck in your ways.

the responsibilities of men and women when they are first dating are very different. Men should do everything they can to make the experience as fun, easy, and entertaining as possible. Women should do everything they can to be flexible, accommodating, and positive at all costs. This way the man and the woman will make determinations about each other based on their true personality traits and looks, not on circumstances. If he tries to set up a really fun date and something goes wrong that is out of his control, don't judge him on that. Appreciate that he did his best to show you a good time, and he'll appreciate that you rolled with the punches.

ask yourself this: Will he think this is cute or crazy? Something that you and your girlfriends think is adorable, he may think is completely nuts so keep the quirks to yourself until you are completely comfortable with the guy. You don't want to scare him off with stories of how you talk to your car or by telling him there is a ghost in your bedroom or that you believe in aliens. There are some things about you he doesn't need to know just yet. This isn't about TMI; you just don't want to seem weird (see rule number one). Wait to reveal those quirky things until you are totally comfortable with him and know that he won't judge you. I'm not saying that you shouldn't be yourself—just make sure to present your quirks so they seem cute, not crazy.

mom says, "If you tell the truth the first time, you won't have to remember what you said." Women often ask us, "Why do men always lie?" And I tell them it's because men think it's easier to get what they want with a lie rather than the truth. If you suspect a man isn't being honest with you, remember that what he is lying about isn't nearly as important as *why* he is lying. If he suddenly cancels plans with you and comes up with a lame excuse, or doesn't call when he said he would, or makes up reasons to avoid meeting your friends and family, it's most important to figure out why he's doing these things. You must not put him on the defensive by accusing him without proof. Try offering solutions to get to the root of the problem. And remember, honesty is always the best policy.

just because you have no idea what's going on doesn't mean you have to look like it. If you are in a group, especially if you are with the friends of a man you are dating, and someone is talking about something you know nothing about, *act* like you know something about it. Appear interested, nod your head, and try to look like you are familiar with the subject. The conversation will eventually move on to something you *are* comfortable discussing, or you can jump in and steer it in any direction you like. After you're out of the conversation, do your research and find out what they were talking about. Then the next time you run into someone from that group you might be able to present a piece of information that shows you know a thing or two about what they're discussing.

"*all work and* no play makes Jack a dull boy." Every guy loves a girl who has goals in life, but don't make it the only topic of discussion. Being proud of what you do, your accomplishments, awards you have won, and honors you have received is one thing, but talking about it incessantly is tiresome. Don't let your career or academic accomplishments become your identity. It's important to have lots of interests, including recreational ones. Be able to tell him what you do for fun; don't appear one-dimensional.

be aware of what you put out there. Mom always says, "Stop and think before you do." You have to think about what you say before you say it because you never know how he might react and how it could impact your connection. It's quite possible you know a lot of the same people, and you might say something offensive about someone he likes or cares about. Remember to be careful not to say anything controversial before you know the guy very well, or you could accidentally insult him and ruin a potential relationship. Also, your stories have to add up. If a man catches you in a lie because you don't have your facts straight, or if he comes to believe you exaggerate or embellish your stories, he won't trust you. If a man doesn't trust you but continues to see you, he won't expect you to trust him . . . and you shouldn't.

enthusiasm is very attractive, especially if you are out of your element. Guys love a girl who is up for anything. The women who can have fun doing anything as long as they are in good company are the keepers. Have passion and energy about whatever you do, but keep it contained, and don't go overboard. Energetic is good, but too bubbly, intense, or excited can be a turnoff. Balance yourself and let him show you the way to enjoy whatever you're doing. If you fake being excited about something he will know it, so be as genuine as possible. Enthusiasm for learning and experiencing life is important in keeping a relationship going. You have to be willing to try new things together.

sex

Be mindful of rushing a connection with someone. Make sure you have the same goals before you are intimate. You may want a relationship when all he wants is to get into your pants. Before you are intimate with him, be clear about what you both want from the relationship. Sex is an extremely personal subject; no two people are exactly alike in their experiences and views of sex. When treated respectfully, openly, and honestly, sex can take your connection to the next level and help you shore up the foundation for a long-lasting relationship. If intimacy is rushed or happens for the wrong reasons, it will likely ruin the connection and could possibly cause emotional scars that will inhibit future relationships. You are the only one who can judge when the time is right for sex.

guys like sexy, not slutty. A slutty girl may be okay for one night, but if you are looking for a lasting relationship, don't be slutty. Being sexy does not mean being naked. To be sexy you must be confident, fun, and approachable. Being sexy is about your look and attitude. It's about drawing a man in, how you carry yourself and how you talk. Being sexy is being inviting, and letting him know that it is okay to approach you. There is a way to be sensual and sexy without being slutty. If you appear to be the kind of girl who will, or does, give it all up on the first date, there will be no reason for him to ask you out again. Giving up sex too easily will devalue you and ruin the excitement and anticipation for him. He should look forward to getting intimate with you when the time is right, not whenever he feels like it. You may think it's a double standard, but the reality is that no guy wants to take that girl home to Mom. Remember, guys love the thrill of the hunt.

if you think having sex with a man means you're automatically going to be in a monogamous relationship, you should check with him first. Don't assume that he's going to be monogamous unless you've actually discussed it. Having the conversation will spare you from ambiguity, frustration, and anger down the road. It is the responsibility of the woman to express herself and state her expectations. You can't assume he knows how you feel unless you spell it out. Obviously, this is not something you bring up on the first date, but it is a conversation you should have before you are intimate with a guy. There is nothing wrong with telling him, "If we're going to sleep together, I expect that you aren't going to sleep with anyone else." Entering into a sexual relationship is like entering into a social contract. It should be discussed and agreed upon by both parties. This doesn't apply only to intimate relationships between a man and a woman; this principle applies to all relationships. What goes on between two people in the privacy of their own homes is no one else's business. As long as there is mutual understanding and respect, you can do whatever you like in your relationship. Communication is the key. He can't read your mind and you can't read his, so don't assume he looks at a situation and sees it the same way you do. Men and women usually see things differently, so it's very important that he understands exactly where you are coming from. That doesn't mean you have to be demanding; just be direct, open, and honest.

For example: You meet a guy you like and he asks you out. You have a great time with him on the first and second dates, and by now you've met some of each other's friends. They approve, and things seem to be going really well. You talk on the phone frequently and he seems interested, but you haven't had sex yet or talked about dating exclusively. Now, imagine you have plans with a friend on a Friday night and she cancels on you at the last minute. The guy you've been seeing knows you were supposed to be busy that night. You don't get in touch with your guy, and decide to go out anyway, to your favorite bar (where you've gone with him before), to hang out since your plans fell through. When you get to the bar you see him there with another girl. Emotions run through you—pain, shock, disappointment, and anger. It could be a very awkward situation. What do you do? You could just leave before he has a chance to see you and ask him what he did that night the next time you see him. If he saw you come in, you could take the high road and go over, say hello, and politely introduce yourself to the woman he's with in a composed manner. You never know—she could be a coworker, or a friend from his hometown. As difficult as it may seem, you can't fault him for seeing another woman, because you did not communicate your expectations. If you had, it would be a totally different story. Guys need this sort of thing spelled out for them. If you don't want him to see or sleep with other people, you need to tell him! So if you really liked this guy and you thought the relationship had potential, you have no justifiable reason to bail out just yet. You should talk to him about it and be clear as to what you want and expect. Communication, respect, and trust are the cornerstones of a lasting relationship.

you've probably heard this before: "Why buy the cow when you can get the milk for free?" Usually it's in reference to getting intimate with a man too quickly, or moving in with him before you're engaged. We like to apply this principle in a broader sense: Don't give away too much of anything too soon. It's important to keep your guy wanting more—more information, more sex, more time with you. Your time is valuable; don't give it away for free!

you hold the cards until you sleep with a man. Use this time to define the boundaries of your relationship. Take things as fast or as slow as you feel comfortable with. The woman determines the pace of the relationship, depending on her goals and the individual situation. You control how rapidly the relationship accelerates. Think of it like a car: Some women are like hot rods and some are more like hybrids. Each car has its pros and cons, but the most important thing to remember is that each should be treated respectfully. The hybrid will be slower, but it is more fuel-efficient, cost-effective, and eco-friendly. The hot rod looks better, and will move much faster, but it burns more gas, is louder, and will definitely be more expensive to maintain. Men must know which type is best for them and then choose their ride accordingly. No matter what, if you're good to both cars they will be good to you. Women must identify what kind of car they are and not try to be something else. If you're a hybrid and pretend to be a hot rod, you'll get nowhere with your man. Be true to yourself, your goals, and your desires. Remember not to mistreat either vehicle, yours or his, because it could cause irreparable damage.

having sex with a guy is a personal decision and depends on the individual circumstances. No matter what, you shouldn't sleep with a guy you want to take you seriously until you have a foundation of communication, respect, and trust. I understand that women have needs; just keep in mind that it's very unlikely you'll have a future with a guy if you sleep with him right away. Men instinctively *want* to pursue women, so you shouldn't end the thrill of the hunt for them prematurely. Typically their goal is to get a woman into bed as soon as possible. It has to do with instant gratification and the idea of accomplishing something that requires time, effort, and focus. That is, they feel outstanding and exceptional if you "don't normally do this." This is why the notion of taking a woman home the night they meet is so gratifying. They like to feel they've bested other men and won the prize with more ease than would be required of others. Although men like their relationships to be easy, they don't want the women they're going into relationships with to be easy. But you shouldn't set up hard and fast rules for when you'll sleep with a guy for the first time, either. Generally, the end of a first date with someone you just met isn't the right time to go home with him, but restricting yourself to a specific timetable will impede the natural flow of the relationship. Like I said, men have to be made to feel exceptional. Even if they can't catch you as quickly as they'd like, sometimes just letting them know how close you are to being caught makes the anticipation and excitement of the catch that much more thrilling. Let your feelings guide you, and have sex only when it feels right. If you're genuinely at a point in your life where you'd rather be in a relationship than be single, before you have sex with someone you should ask yourself if you are ready to take that step toward a relationship with him. Is he someone you could see yourself getting serious with? Could it be a long-term thing? If the answer is yes, go for it.

you must stroke your man's . . . ego. Men have to feel special. They must feel wanted *and* needed, and for many women this is much trickier than it sounds. When a man flirts, takes you out, or is doing something he is proud of (especially sex), you have to recognize the effort and give him positive reinforcement. You always have to let him know when you're enjoying yourself and when he's doing something right. Never point out what he is doing wrong, whether it's too fast or too slow or too soft or too hard. Just subtly change the course of things yourself, or introduce positive reinforcement by saying, "Let me try this," or "It feels so good when you . . ." For guys, sex is remarkably and intricately bound to the ego. Men have to think they are doing a good job. You don't have to fake orgasms, but if he does something you really like, make sure you give the guy an "attaboy!"

Sexual communication is critical. It's not the place for exaggeration or mixed signals, but with the right amount of encouragement you can only make it better for both of you.

think of sex before a relationship like selling a luxury car. As the dealer, you want to attract the right buyer, so you put out signs everywhere advertising your cars and services and hope the right buyer comes in soon. Being the inviting, friendly dealer that you are, you have a great lot and a beautiful showroom that will intrigue and attract shoppers. When a qualified buyer expresses interest in one of your cars, you may let him take the car out for a spin—but you'd never let him open it up on the highway at 140 mph, or take it home with him. If a woman has sex with a man before they are in a committed relationship, she should never pull out all the stops. In other words, never do all the things you'd be comfortable doing in a relationship, or else he'll have nothing to look forward to. Trust me on this. Mastering the delicate art of timing could pay dividends for the rest of your love life.

guys are turned off by a woman's sexual past, so don't talk about your previous exploits. Most men are bright enough to realize that you're probably not a virgin, and they definitely don't want to know exactly how experienced you are or how you became so good. Let them think you're just a natural. As far as a man is concerned, he's the very first guy you've ever slept with. You probably don't want to hear all about his past sexual experiences, either, and trust me—he really doesn't want to hear about yours. The smartest, safest, and soundest thing to do is for both of you to get checked out before you sleep together. Some men rationalize that even after having slept with innumerable women, if they get tested and have a clean bill of health physically, they're cleaner than a whistle and no different than a virgin. Obviously, women don't look at it that way. Don't ask me why, but it's different for men and women, so always remember to be safe and responsible.

developing

You begin to turn a connection into a commitment only after you've dated long enough to know you want to see each other more often and you agree to be exclusive. During the development stage you start introducing him to friends and family, taking trips together, discussing the future, and investing more time, energy, and effort into the commitment.

it's important to reveal yourself carefully when you're dating someone, but you can reveal yourself more freely once you're developing a relationship. When first dating, create a sense of mystery so he becomes intrigued with you; he'll want to see you again and again to learn more about you and your life. You don't want to be a completely open book at first. But as you become more familiar with the guy, only reveal more when you're confident he won't make snap judgments and will consider everything he knows about you before drawing conclusions. Then you'll be able to share more personal details about your life. Sharing personal information at the right time is critical to the development of a relationship.

friends don't let friends date bitches. If you seem high-maintenance, obnoxious, confrontational, or combative to his friends, they can and will turn him against you very easily. If his friends tell him they don't like you or they've seen him with hotter girls than you, it could spell the end of your relationship. Men are like women in this regard: They value the opinions of people who matter to them. Just be confident and friendly. If, over time, you find you really don't click with his crowd, he may not be the right guy for you. If you don't like one or two of your boyfriend's friends but the relationship is important enough that you decide to deal with it, try to find something positive about those friends and focus on that. You have to find the good in them. If you can't, you're just going to have to pretend to like them. Because if you can't get along with them you will put him in a position of having to spend time with you and his friends separately, and no matter what, that will mean less time for the two of you. If he starts keeping his time with you and his friends separate and his buddies know you don't like them, they'll do whatever they can to poison the well and get him to break up with you. Don't bring unnecessary tension into a developing relationship by stirring up trouble with his friends. And don't expect him to get rid of them. A man will love it if you fit in with the guys and everyone can hang out together. When meeting friends or family it is important not to disrupt the harmony of the group. You should try to fit in with the pack. Make the group feel comfortable around you, and be comfortable around them. Remember, you *are* the company you keep, and this rule applies to both the man and the woman. And when you introduce him to your friends, keep in mind that they are a reflection of you. He'll try to assess whether or not he can be friends with them, or at least spend time with them, just as you did with his friends.

if you take him seriously enough to introduce him to your friends and family, you have to be mindful of how you represent him to them, and vice versa. Perception, preconceived notions, and first impressions are critical to keeping the support of the people you care about most. Do your best to speak positively about him to them, and about them to him. When you represent him to your friends and family, sing his praises and highlight what you like most about him. If you've been dating a guy for a while and you're constantly on the phone with your mom telling her only the bad things he does—how he's always late, doesn't call you back, etc.—she's not going to like him. The relationship may be going well, and there may be more positive than negative, but if you focus only on the bad stuff, she's not going to have a very high opinion of him. Try not to create a negative impression before your friends and family actually get to know the guy. Women tend to pick apart a relationship even when it's going well, so if you find yourself doing this, remind yourself to try to focus on the positive. Nurture your friends' and family's perception of him. Don't sabotage it. Also, prepare him for who he is about to meet. Try to make it a little easier for him. Don't try to out-think love, or overthink your relationship. It can be hard for women to do this, but try not to overanalyze everything. Make sure he's on the same page as you in terms of what you think and how you feel about the relationship. Sometimes the most difficult questions have the simplest answers, so don't make things more complicated than they have to be. Be practical when developing a relationship. If you have doubts, get a second opinion from a trusted friend or a professional (like your matchmaker), but try not to involve all of your girlfriends and pour out every little detail about the relationship. Trust me; he's not doing that with the guys.

don't second-guess the relationship, and try to relax. If he's communicating, sharing, and being thoughtful, you're on the right track. If you've been single for a while and have met a great guy who wants to see you more, don't think _This is too good to be true; I'm sure there's something wrong._ Once you've made it clear that you're seeing just each other, the worst thing you can do is make him think you're having doubts or trust issues.

planning too far ahead spells pressure for a guy. Bringing up marriage, kids, and a ten-year plan is not a good idea unless he brings these things up first. If he's not the dreamer type who talks about the future and you bring this stuff up first, he'll think your biological clock is ticking like a stopwatch. As you get to know him better, details about his ambitions and plans for the future will emerge naturally, so try not to force it.

most men are uncomfortable with public displays of affection (PDA), so don't be too touchy-feely in front of others. People stare at this behavior because it is inappropriate. It's okay to be a little affectionate, like holding hands or putting your arms around each other. That's fine. But don't make other people uncomfortable, and be aware of your surroundings. If spectators are yelling, "Get a room!" you know you've gone too far in public.

don't take yourself too seriously. Learn how to make light of situations that might make you uncomfortable or seemingly look bad. Learn to laugh at yourself. If something goes wrong on a date or in your relationship, it's not the end of the world. Try to put it in perspective and realize that others have gone through what you're going through before. Music is often a great way to find comfort in dealing with whatever emotional challenges you face when you're dating, developing, or moving on from a relationship.

learn to let things go. If a potential relationship doesn't work out, a guy doesn't call you back, or you're otherwise disappointed by men, you have to learn to let it go and put it behind you. Don't be negative. Put the effort you would take to complain about it into finding another relationship if you're ready, willing, and able to be in one. Bringing bad blood into a budding relationship will only turn a guy off and make him feel like he has to work harder than he ought to just to get you over whatever resentment or bitterness you're harboring.

don't dismiss a guy just because he lives in another city. Long-distance relationships can work, but when dealing with distance the relationship's viability depends much more on the quality of the time you spend together than the quantity. Make the most of the time you have to be with him and do things you don't normally do, even if that means doing touristy things in the town you live in. Go sightseeing; visit aquariums, zoos, parks, and museums; attend sporting events, the opera, and charity events; etc. Travel to places neither of you goes to often or has been to before. Eventually one of you will have to make the move to make it work. If the relationship is getting stronger and the commitment is there, it's okay to discuss a plan of action and to do your best to make it happen.

unless he gives you a reason not to trust him, you shouldn't be suspicious. Don't get paranoid! Guys don't want to feel like they're under surveillance. Jealousy shows your insecurity and, in some cases, can make a guy second-guess being with you. Then he may just start looking elsewhere. Be confident in your relationship and face your fears, but don't jump to conclusions. If you have legitimate reasons to believe he's lying to you or seeing someone else when the relationship is supposed to be exclusive, approach him directly. Don't be passive-aggressive or confrontational. Offer him an easy way out of the relationship. If he doesn't take it, then restate your expectations and tell him you need more assurance from him from time to time that he's as committed to the relationship as you are. The relationships that last are based on trust and honesty. You have to keep the lines of communication open.

don't make mountains out of molehills or get worked up over things that happened in the past. Resist googling the women he's been with before if you are curious about them. Don't keep pictures or mementos of your exes around, either. When you go from dating someone to being in a relationship with him, you don't have to get rid of these things permanently, or expect him to, either, but you should at least put them somewhere he won't find them—and he should do the same for you. Often, if a woman even sees a picture of the girl he was with before her, her mind will spin. She will start questioning whether the ex is prettier or skinnier, or has better clothes, hair, style, etc. Even bothering to think about your guy and his ex could completely derail your developing relationship. Don't compare yourself to her. He's not with her anymore. He's with you. Be confident and respect the history they share just as you would hope he would do for you. Each individual has their own tolerance level when it comes to exes, so know your limits and understand that dealing with exes is part of the relationship-building process. Guys will compare themselves to your exes sexually before anything else. It has to do with virility, potency, and pride. The door swings both ways, and he will go through emotions similar to the ones you experience. In general, concerning yourself with an ex is never a good idea, so don't talk about yours or his when dating, or even once you're in a relationship. Even couples who are happily married don't want to hear about their partners' pasts. It's important for the other person to feel you're emotionally detached from anyone in your past. He should never question whether you might go back with an ex. He needs to know there is *no* chance of reconciliation with anyone you were ever with. When it comes to ex-spouses, former mates, and any lasting ties you might share, such as children, alimony, property settlements, etc., these matters must seem manageable, tolerable, and under control. Remind him that you're with him now, and the past is in the past.

there comes a time in any developing relationship when you have to tell each other certain things in order to strengthen the bond between you. The key to doing this effectively is to convey your negative need-to-know experiences as positively as possible. Emphasize what you've learned from them and how they've helped you grow. Beware of what you tell him, when you tell him, why you tell him, and how you tell him. It sounds stressful, but the only thing I can tell you is to trust your instincts. If it is the right time to talk about whatever it is you need to discuss, it will be an issue only if you make an issue of it. If you have things like anxiety, financial distress, depression, ADD, children, or any number of things to deal with but you deal with them well, he should understand. But if you pick the wrong time to tell him something important, it could backfire, and instead of bringing you closer it could scare him away. You must reveal need-to-know information when you're confident he can handle it. Be sure to present things in a way that focuses on how they've made you a better, more self-aware person. Communication is the key to moving a relationship forward, so be sure that you are communicating honestly and responsibly.

religion and spirituality are two of the most slippery slopes in dating and developing relationships. These are the double black diamonds of love. To make it down these trails safely you have to be extremely careful. First and foremost, it's important to believe in something, and to be able to explain why you believe. Believing in nothing still amounts to believing in something if you have conviction and even the slightest amount of interest in or explanation for how we got here and what's in store for mankind. Whether you were born and raised Jewish, Christian, Muslim, Hindu, Buddhist, or anything else, you have to have strength in your beliefs and be willing to justify them at the right time. If your religion is different from his and you can respectfully agree to disagree, the relationship could still work. You don't have to have the same religious beliefs, but you must have the same values, morals, and principles.

often, one's family's influence can add pressure when dating and building relationships. If he doesn't fit in with your family, it could be a dealbreaker. It's important to understand where someone comes from and what his values are before letting the relationship get serious only to find it doesn't work out because your families drive you apart. I've seen many occasions where two people who were deeply in love didn't get married because of family conflict when it came to how to raise children, celebrate holidays, carry on traditions, etc. Once you've moved past dating and are developing a serious relationship with someone you must be clear about whatever obstacles there might be regarding your family. If you love each other enough you may be able to compromise in a way that will satisfy everyone and still allow the relationship to evolve. Overcoming obstacles that involve family could also bring a couple closer together. Family and religion are hurdles that many couples have to overcome, because these are usually make-or-break issues. The most important thing to remember when dealing with family and religion is to be sensitive, respectful, and understanding. Insensitivity when it comes to family or religion on any level could doom a relationship.

mom always told me, "You'll never know until you have kids of your own one day," and I've always respected that. If you don't have kids and are with someone who does, remember that his children are his first commitment. If he has children and you disagree with how he raises them sometimes, or how his ex handles them, keep your opinions to yourself unless the child seems to be in danger. When you are developing a relationship with someone is not the time to criticize his parenting skills, but it *is* a good time to discuss how you feel about kids of your own. Do you like kids, love them, simply tolerate them, or can't stand them? Is he the guy to start a family with if you don't like the way he's raising his kids? Once again, this is an issue where the door swings both ways. You may be a single mom starting to develop a relationship with someone who doesn't have children. In this case it's very important to let a man know that although your children are your first priority, a very close second is to be in a healthy, happy relationship. Make sure you let him know that you have support from people around you so that you can still do things like a romantic getaway or three-day weekend or, at the very least, an occasional overnight somewhere. Men need to know they are important to you. They have to feel both wanted and needed. Be sure you're mindful of this if there are kids in the picture. For example, if a child gets sick and you have to cancel your date, or if your child got in trouble at school and you need to be home to discipline him, the man must know that you'll want to make it up to him and that you actually do have the time to be in a relationship. This also goes for any other obligations or priorities that may impede a relationship, such as career, family, community service, charity work, volunteering, extracurricular activities, travel, etc.

keeping and maintaining

Keeping and maintaining a relationship is just as difficult as developing one in the first place. You may think that you already have him, so all the work is done, but you're wrong. If you think like that you could very well lose him faster than you landed him. Keeping the spark of excitement in your relationship is critical to making it last. Don't take him for granted because you managed to marry him or move in with him. Instead, you should realize how lucky you are to be in a healthy, happy relationship and do everything you can to nurture it together.

when you are in a relationship (and this applies to any sort of relationship), take a moment to collect yourself and avoid a fight. Calm yourself down before you do or say something you might regret later. If you say something spiteful you can't just take it back, even if you didn't mean it. If what you said or did is really hurtful, he may eventually forgive you, but he will never forget—especially if it insults his pride, ego, or intelligence. You may make up and think everything is fine, but the hurt will linger. Before a fight escalates, take a step back and agree to discuss things when you both calm down. This may be a little easier for him than for you because women often want to address a problem right away and talk about how it makes them feel. Men usually want to just solve the problem and avoid any emotional discussion if possible. Make it clear you're just taking a break from things to get a grip, give him a kiss, and walk away. Remind yourself of all the positive things about your relationship and why you love him. Then maybe the fight won't seem as important. Remember to try to stay in control. You don't want to be a screaming mess and say something nasty, because he may forgive you for it, but he won't forget.

tell him how good he makes you feel. Whether you've been married for twenty years or it's the first time you've been with him, you should always tell him how great he makes you feel. Tell him he's the best lover you ever had. If he isn't or you don't feel comfortable making that statement, you could always say something just as flattering, like, "Wow, you're so amazing!" or "I needed that so bad, thank you!" Whether you've told him a thousand times before or not even once, this is the sort of thing men can't get enough of, and men love to hear it again and again. Just as you expect him to keep the relationship fresh and exciting, you have to do your part as well. Nothing motivates a man more than an "attaboy!" It's important to express how much you care about your man. Don't get so comfortable that he thinks you take him for granted. We all know you wouldn't want him to make you feel that way.

avoid growing apart.

When you are in a relationship, you have to train yourself to grow together. Think of the relationship like a bonsai tree—one branch may grow quicker than another, or in a different direction, but the whole tree still grows together. Just like a bonsai, you need to trim and shape the relationship in order for it to grow in the direction you want. You must make sure the branches are growing together. For example, say a couple gets married young and has kids right away. The wife stays home to care for the kids and run the household. Her husband works outside of the home. She's your typical soccer mom. He is devoted to his wife and their children, but their relationship centers around the kids and their activities. The couple figures that once the kids are grown and out of the house, they'll have time to travel and enjoy their independence together. Years pass. The kids leave for college and the husband is now eager to start planning trips and doing all the things they put off while raising their kids. But the wife has become so accustomed to her space and her environment that she's reluctant to go anywhere. She's not as adventurous as she was when she first met her husband, and they suddenly realize that they have almost nothing in common anymore other than, of course, their children. This is the sort of thing that can be avoided if each person takes the time to focus on their individual growth and the growth of the relationship. It's not easy when you're busy with a career and raising a family, but it's critical to making a relationship last.

the key to keeping a relationship going strong is to use diplomacy before war. You will sometimes have to agree to disagree for the greater good of the relationship. Go to whatever lengths are necessary to always put the other person first. If each person in the relationship concentrates on putting the other first, the only possible outcome is love and happiness. However, in order for this to work, both people have to think this way. Never try to one-up each other in a relationship—love is not a competition. Quite the contrary; resigning yourself to the other person's happiness is an expression of love. Avoid battling with each other at all costs. It will only breed discontent and resentment that will fester over time and ultimately bring about the demise of the relationship. Remember to look at the big picture. Pick your battles carefully, and expend your time and energy in positive ways.

my mom always taught me that when you're in a relationship you should never go to bed angry. This may sound cliché, but it's true. Don't let arguments linger, or end the day on a negative note. Even if you are angry at each other, remember that you love each other. Arguments can get extremely emotional and blown out of proportion very easily. Be careful not to say anything you may regret. Don't waste your time being angry. It's much easier for women to communicate and want to resolve an issue, so more often than not you're going to have to be the peacekeeper. Keep things in perspective; if the fight lingers it will just get worse and worse.

at some point in life everyone gets rejected somehow. Learn from each experience and move on—you will be a better person for it. There is someone out there for you, so don't give up! When you do find love, you will realize it was worth all the effort along the way.

conclusion

All of the principles and advice we're giving you may seem intimidating. It's a lot to remember, and it's a lot to think about, but it's really not all that complicated. Dating is training. It's conditioning. And practice makes perfect. If you practice these principles you'll perfect your love life—it's really that simple. Use the guidelines that apply to you and remember that every relationship, every date, every single connection is circumstantial and unique, so there will be times when some of these rules may not apply. You have to be a problem-solver. You may not have a problem meeting guys, but if the chemistry doesn't last past the third date, or you're repeatedly disappointed by men, or you make the same mistakes over and over again, then you're doing something wrong and only you can fix it. In every case, evaluate what you are doing, how you are carrying yourself, and what you're talking about, and then try some of our tips. Do something different. You can't keep doing the same thing and expect different results. If you are not ending up with the right guys, change your strategy, change your approach, and change where you're going—but you don't have to change who you are. If you are having trouble finding guys, start looking elsewhere. There are men everywhere! And men really don't care where or how they meet a woman if there's chemistry. A guy will strike up a conversation anywhere if you seem approachable.

Women tell us all the time that they don't want to be approached at a gym because they are there to work out; they aren't looking to meet a man when they're on a treadmill. But look at it from a man's perspective: If he thinks you look good covered in sweat, with no makeup on, in gym clothes, and with your hair in a ponytail, just imagine how blown away he'll be when he sees you with your hair blown out, in heels, and rocking your favorite little black dress. Most women in happy relationships tell me they met someone when they least expected it, so it stands to reason that if you try to be more self-aware in situations where you wouldn't normally expect to meet someone, you may notice that the perfect guy is right under your nose. Your true love could be in front of you in line at the grocery store, or he could be your newest neighbor in your building. He could be ordering a cup of coffee a few feet away from you while you're reading this book in your favorite café. Why eliminate anyone, anywhere, anytime if he could be the right fit for you? We've matched countless couples who were reluctant to meet and had to be convinced to go out with each other. Once they got over their hang-ups and realized that all their preconceived notions were unfounded and irrelevant, however, their relationships flourished. Usually the person you end up with is not the person you might've imagined yourself with. That's why we call them fantasies in the first place. Just remember to focus on being yourself and the best you can be.

It's okay to work on yourself before you jump into any relationship, and dating is the perfect way to do that—especially if you can get feedback and learn some things about yourself in the process. The best way to attract a man is to constantly work on improving yourself in any way necessary, whether it's by working out, dealing with family issues, getting your career together, or something entirely different. If you do this you can be certain that you will exude confidence when you meet someone new.

Think of dating and ending up in a relationship like sneaking a peek at a Christmas present before opening it on Christmas morning. You're the gift he's been waiting for. He sees you as a package wrapped so beautifully he can barely wait to open it. When he picks it up his mind will be racing, just imagining the possibilities of what's inside. He'll feel like he's going to burst with anticipation, imagining all the fantastic things that await him. He'll shake it just a little, hoping for a clue to what's inside, but he'll enjoy the excitement of waiting because once he unwraps the present, it's finally his and there is no rewrapping it or putting it back under the tree. There's no gift receipt. There's no way to exchange it for something else. He may be thrilled with what he got, but then again, he may also be disappointed. You are opening a present as well, and the same applies to you. Even if your gift turns out to be not exactly what you hoped for or what you expected, you should still appreciate it. Make the best of each relationship you're in and treat it as a gift. Try to learn something from every relationship you have and every man who comes and goes in your life. What you learn from these experiences may ultimately be what leads you to the one you're meant to end up with.

Manage your fears and live in faith. Try not to let your insecurities hold you back from finding, developing, and maintaining a healthy, happy relationship. When you first meet someone your fears will be based more on looks, appearances, and impressions than anything else. You may be nervous about what other people will think of him and the idea of the two of you in a relationship. As the connection strengthens, those fears will subside, but more personal and potentially damaging ones may arise. You will have fears based on his experiences and your experiences and what you each have learned from them. Maybe he cheated on an ex and you worry that means he'll cheat on you. Maybe he switches jobs frequently and you question his stability. You may have seen him angry, or maybe he doesn't have the same beliefs as you. These fears are more intrinsic and more personal, but they can be overcome. Once a commitment has been made, the fears become about losing that commitment. The only way to battle your fears in all stages of a relationship is to live with complete faith in life and love. You have to believe in this person, and believe you can have a successful life with him. Fear is, quite simply, the absence of faith. Having complete faith in another person is love in real life, and the more faith you have the more love you live—and the stronger your connection will be.

Don't be afraid to take chances. Remember, what doesn't kill you will make you stronger. It may be hard, and there may be heartache along the way, but if you don't keep trying you'll never find that truly special connection.

glossary

commitment: Commitment is the understanding and expectation to be present, invested, and involved in all matters important to each other.

connection: A connection is what binds two people together like pieces of a puzzle. Everything is predicated on the connection. The stronger the connection between two people, the easier it is to overcome the challenges they'll face in their relationship. A connection is organic, and it ebbs and flows. It can become stronger and weaker, and stronger again over time. To keep a connection strong takes effort and commitment. A connection is caused by a force that draws people together like magnetism, but it must be nurtured and nourished to last.

love (according to JoAnn): Love is being willing to sacrifice for another person and always finding a way to compromise with them. If you're willing to make sacrifices and put them before yourself, you are in love.

love (according to Steve): When you love someone it means you've suspended your own ego whenever you're with them. You are defenseless and ego-less around them. The force that makes a connection is love, but there are degrees of love. Loving someone does not mean that you are *in* love. I love my friends, and I have a connection with them, but I'm not *in* love with them. There are many dimensions to love.

lust: Lust is the sensual reaction to physical attraction. It is a one-dimensional sexual attraction.

lust vs. love: Men will lust first. They are visual creatures and will react to a physical attraction in a very one-dimensional way. To build a relationship on lust without communication, respect, and trust will result in a purely physical relationship with no emotional attachment. Lust can be confused with what love really feels like. When you lust after someone and have sex right away, you make it more difficult to develop a relationship on an emotional level. You can't build healthy relationships on just good sex. If lust takes over too soon and you're intimate too quickly, you're letting a man get away with getting all the perks of a relationship without getting invested emotionally.

making love vs. having sex: When you are having sex with a person with whom you've formed a foundation of communication, respect, and trust, and your goal is their satisfaction before your own, then you are making love with them. Having sex doesn't require an emotional connection. It is a plain and simple pleasure-seeking act. To make love, you need to have the connection with that person and want to love them.

romance: Romance is often considered a catalyst for a love connection. Men use romance to demonstrate how considerate and appreciative they can be. Sending flowers, making a candlelit dinner, blocking everyone else out for a night and just focusing on the person you're with so you can create a memorable moment is romantic. Being thoughtful is romantic, but being romantic isn't always thoughtful. Romance can be selfish if the motive is sex or peace and quiet, but thoughtfulness is completely selfless.

thoughtfulness: Showing your partner you took the time to consider their needs and are willing to go out of your way for them is being thoughtful. Examples of a man showing thoughtfulness are calling on his way home to ask if you need anything, or getting up a few minutes early to walk the dog so you don't have to. Thoughtfulness is bringing flowers home for no reason other than to see the smile on your face. It could be something big or something not big at all. It's a gesture. Thoughtfulness keeps a relationship going strong, and it goes hand in hand with communication and respect. It's a factor of love. Two people cannot sustain a love connection without thoughtfulness and the willingness to go out of their way for each other. The opposite of thoughtfulness is selfishness.

About the Authors

STEVE WARD is the host of the VH1 hit reality show *Tough Love* and CEO of Master Matchmakers, an exclusive matchmaking service founded by his mother, JoAnn.

JoANN WARD, a happily married mother of three adult children, is the founder and president of Master Matchmakers, which has been successfully connecting single men and women for more than twenty years. She is a frequent guest star on VH1's *Tough Love*.

Printed in the United States
By Bookmasters